101 Life-Changing Chinese Proverbs

Wisdom from Ancient China, Translated and Explained

101 Life-Changing Chinese Proverbs: *Wisdom from Ancient China, Translated and Explained*

© [16/06/2025] [Maxwell W. Wilson]

Cover design by Timothy Brooks

ISBN: [9798288305986]

Disclaimer : *This book is for informational purposes only. While every effort has been made to ensure the accuracy and completeness of the information contained herein, the author and publisher assume no responsibility for errors, inaccuracies, omissions, or any outcomes resulting from the use of this information. The content is provided on an "as-is" basis and does not constitute professional or technical advice. Readers are encouraged to consult official sources and professionals for specific guidance.*

Trademarks : *All brand names and product names used in this book are trademarks, registered trademarks, or trade names of their respective holders. The use of trademarks is for reference only and does not imply any affiliation with or endorsement by the trademark holders.*

For permissions, media inquiries, or publishing opportunities, please contact the author at: sspider1012@gmail.com

路漫漫其修远兮，吾将上下而求索

Lù mànmàn qí xiūyuǎn xī, wú jiāng shàngxià ér qiúsuǒ

The road ahead is long and has no ending; yet high and low I will search with my will unbending.

Qu Yuan (屈原), from Li Sao (离骚), 3rd century BCE

To the quiet wisdom of my ancestors,
To the patient teachers who spoke without words,
And to every reader who seeks meaning in the old to better
live the new.

There is a stillness to ancient wisdom. It doesn't hurry to reveal itself, nor does it clamor for attention. It waits—silent, patient—like water shaping stone or a mountain holding the memory of seasons. Chinese proverbs are born from this stillness. They are brief, but not shallow. Sparse, but not empty. Their power lies not in their length, but in their depth.

This book is the fruit of years of quiet listening.

I didn't set out to write a book of Chinese proverbs. I came across one, by accident, in a conversation. Then another, folded into a line of poetry. Then a third, whispered by an old film, or scribbled in the corner of a calligraphy scroll. Each one struck me—not like a hammer, but like a bell. The words would echo inside me, long after they were spoken. I began to gather them. And as I did, I realized that I wasn't merely collecting phrases—I was unearthing a worldview.

These proverbs—some drawn from Confucian teachings, others from Daoist texts, Buddhist reflections, and folk sayings passed down through generations—offer not rules, but reflections. They don't instruct so much as invite. They are not blunt instruments of advice, but subtle companions for those willing to pause and ponder.

They speak of balance, patience, time, humility, and the art of living lightly but fully. In them, you'll find rivers and stones, the moon and wind, distant drums of ancestral memory, and soft footprints of daily wisdom left in the snow. Some may guide you through personal storms; others may simply make you smile in recognition.

Each entry in this collection is presented with its original Chinese script, Romanized pinyin for pronunciation, an English translation, and an interpretation. The explanations are meant not to exhaust the meaning, but to open a door. The rest, I trust, you'll walk through on your own.

In curating this volume, I prioritized proverbs that stir something beneath the surface. Not just clever lines or motivational snippets, but those that gently reshape the way we move through the world. Many are poetic. Many are paradoxical. Some are sharp with irony; others, soft with compassion. All are worth living with.

This book is part of the series *Proverbial Wisdom Through the Ages*, where I gather the quiet voices of the past—Latin, Greek, Japanese, Sanskrit, and now Chinese—and let them speak again in the present. My hope is not to make them modern, but to make them heard.

To the thoughtful reader, I offer this: read these proverbs slowly. Return to them often. Not every saying will change your life. But a few might. And sometimes, all it takes is one.

塞翁失马·焉知非福

Sàiwēng shīmǎ, yān zhī fēi fú

When the old man lost his horse, how could one know it was not a blessing?

Life's setbacks often disguise future blessings. This ancient proverb reminds us that fortune and misfortune are fluid—what appears to be a loss may become gain in time. Patience reveals the true shape of events.

千里之行，始于足下

Qiānlǐ zhī xíng, shǐ yú zú xià

A journey of a thousand miles begins beneath your feet. Attributed to Laozi, this proverb teaches that all great undertakings begin with a single, humble step. It encourages courage, initiative, and mindfulness in beginning.

滴水穿石，非一日之功

Dīshuǐ chuān shí, fēi yī rì zhī gōng

Dripping water wears through stone—not in one day's work.

Consistent, patient effort can overcome the greatest obstacles. This saying speaks to the transformative power of perseverance.

知足者常乐

Zhīzú zhě cháng lè

The one who knows contentment is always happy.

Happiness comes not from endless desire but from gratitude and moderation. A call to inner peace through appreciating enough.

君子和而不同

Jūnzǐ hé ér bù tóng

A noble person is in harmony with others, yet not identical to them.

True wisdom lies in unity without uniformity. Respecting differences while maintaining harmony is the mark of virtue.

纸上得来终觉浅，绝知此事要躬行

Zhǐ shàng dé lái zhōng jué qiǎn, jué zhī cǐ shì yào gōng xíng

What is learned from books remains shallow; to truly understand, one must practice it personally.

Theory must be lived to become real wisdom. Experience is the final teacher.

不怕慢，就怕站

Bù pà màn, jiù pà zhàn

Do not fear slow progress—only fear standing still.

Progress, however slow, is still forward motion. Stagnation is the true danger.

己所不欲，勿施于人

Jǐ suǒ bù yù, wù shī yú rén

Do not do to others what you would not want done to yourself.

A cornerstone of Confucian ethics, this golden rule teaches empathy, respect, and restraint.

前事不忘，后事之师

Qián shì bù wàng, hòu shì zhī shī

Past events, if not forgotten, serve as teachers for the future.

History and memory are guides. Mistakes become instruction, and reflection brings wisdom.

大智若愚

Dà zhì ruò yú

Great wisdom appears foolish.

Truly wise people often appear simple or unassuming. This saying challenges superficial judgments and reminds us that depth often hides beneath modesty.

山不厌高，水不厌深

Shān bù yàn gāo, shuǐ bù yàn shēn

The mountain is not tired of its height; the river is not tired of its depth.

A metaphor for excellence and the endless pursuit of growth. True greatness does not rest on its laurels.

良药苦口利于病，忠言逆耳利于行

Liáng yào kǔ kǒu lì yú bìng, zhōng yán nì ěr lì yú xíng

Good medicine tastes bitter but cures illness; honest advice offends the ear but benefits action.

Truth is often hard to accept, but necessary for growth. Accepting difficult truths is a mark of strength.

言多必失

Yán duō bì shī

He who speaks too much is bound to make mistakes.
Sometimes wisdom lies in silence. Speaking less allows for
better listening and fewer regrets.

宁为鸡口，无为牛后

Nìng wéi jī kǒu, wú wéi niú hòu

Better to be the beak of a chicken than the tail of a cow.
It's better to be a leader in a small role than a follower in a
big one. Value autonomy and meaningful position over
status.

水能载舟，亦能覆舟

Shuǐ néng zài zhōu, yì néng fù zhōu

Water can carry a boat—it can also overturn it.
Power, like the people or the environment, can support or
destroy. Balance and respect are crucial to stability.

种瓜得瓜，种豆得豆

Zhòng guā dé guā, zhòng dòu dé dòu

Plant melons, get melons; plant beans, get beans.
You reap what you sow. Actions have consequences—
choose wisely.

蚍蜉撼树，可笑不自量

Pífú hàn shù, kěxiào bù zì liàng

An ant trying to shake a tree—laughable overestimation.
One must recognize one's limits. Overconfidence without awareness invites ridicule and failure.

鱼与熊掌，不可兼得

Yú yǔ xióngzhǎng, bù kě jiān dé

You can't have both the fish and the bear's paw.
Sometimes life demands choices between two desirable things. Wisdom lies in discernment and sacrifice.

一寸光阴一寸金，寸金难买寸光阴

Yī cùn guāngyīn yī cùn jīn, cùn jīn nán mǎi cùn guāngyīn

An inch of time is worth an inch of gold—but you can't buy that inch of time with gold.
Time is precious and irreplaceable. Use it wisely, for once lost, it cannot be reclaimed.

听其言而观其行

Tīng qí yán ér guān qí xíng

Listen to his words but watch his actions.

Words are easy; actions reveal character. Trust should be earned through consistency.

桃李不言，下自成蹊

Táo lǐ bù yán, xià zì chéng qī
Peach and plum trees do not speak, yet a path forms beneath them.
True virtue and excellence need no advertisement—people are naturally drawn to genuine goodness. Influence flows quietly from character, not charisma.

夜长梦多

Yè cháng mèng duō
When the night is long, dreams are many.
When situations are drawn out, uncertainty and complications multiply. A warning against delay and indecision.

一叶障目，不见泰山

Yī yè zhàng mù, bù jiàn Tài Shān
A single leaf before the eye obscures Mount Tai.
Small things can blind us to greater truths. Perspective matters—don't let the trivial eclipse the profound.

风无常顺，兵无常胜

Fēng wú cháng shùn, bīng wú cháng shèng

The wind does not always blow favorably; no army always wins.

Change is constant, and success is never guaranteed. This proverb urges humility in victory and resilience in loss.

螳螂捕蝉，黄雀在后

Tángláng bǔ chán, huángquè zài hòu

The mantis stalks the cicada, unaware of the oriole behind.

There's always a bigger player. Be aware of hidden dangers while pursuing your goals. A classic lesson in caution.

不入虎穴，焉得虎子

Bù rù hǔxué, yān dé hǔzǐ

How can one get a tiger cub without entering the tiger's den?

Great rewards require great risks. Courage is essential to achievement.

水滴石穿，绳锯木断

Shuǐ dī shí chuān, shéng jù mù duàn

Dripping water can wear through stone; a rope can saw through wood.
Repeated effort overcomes all obstacles. This variation reinforces perseverance in the face of difficulty.

覆水难收

Fù shuǐ nán shōu

Spilt water is hard to recover.
Some actions cannot be undone. This proverb is a sober reminder to act with care and foresight.

欲速则不达

Yù sù zé bù dá

Desiring speed leads to failure.
Haste makes waste. Rushing undermines true success. A call to patient, steady progress.

当局者迷，旁观者清

Dāng jú zhě mí, páng guān zhě qīng

The one playing the game is confused; the onlooker sees clearly.

Being too close to a situation clouds judgment. Distance brings clarity. Often, others see what we cannot.

良禽择木而栖

Liáng qín zé mù ér qī

A fine bird chooses the tree it nests in.

The wise choose their environment carefully. This proverb emphasizes discernment in where—and with whom—we align ourselves.

宁可枝头抱香死，不随落叶归尘土

Nìng kě zhī tóu bào xiāng sǐ, bù suí luò yè guī chén tǔ

Better to die with fragrance upon the branch than fall to dust like a leaf.

Integrity and dignity are worth preserving even in the face of death. A poetic call to live—and end—honorably.

三思而后行

Sān sī ér hòu xíng

Think thrice before you act.

Deliberation protects from regret. Careful thinking must precede decisive action.

人无远虑，必有近忧

Rén wú yuǎn lǜ, bì yǒu jìn yōu

He who has no long-term plans will face short-term worries.

Planning is protection. Without foresight, even today becomes troubled.

画蛇添足

Huà shé tiān zú

To draw a snake and add legs.

Overdoing something ruins it. Know when to stop, and when simplicity is best.

树欲静而风不止，子欲养而亲不待

Shù yù jìng ér fēng bù zhǐ, zǐ yù yǎng ér qīn bù dài

The tree wishes to be still, but the wind won't stop; the child wishes to care, but the parents are gone.

A sorrowful reminder to cherish loved ones while they are alive. Opportunities do not wait forever.

宁为玉碎，不为瓦全

Nìng wéi yù suì, bù wéi wǎ quán

Better to be shattered jade than intact pottery.

It is nobler to die with honor than to live in disgrace. A proverb rooted in moral courage.

江山易改，本性难移

Jiāngshān yì gǎi, běnxìng nán yí

Rivers and mountains may change; a person's nature is hard to alter.

True character is deeply ingrained. This serves as both a warning and a call for cautious trust.

势如破竹

Shì rú pò zhú

Like breaking through bamboo.

Used to describe unstoppable momentum, especially in war or business. Once a breakthrough begins, resistance crumbles quickly.

一失足成千古恨

Yī shī zú chéng qiān gǔ hèn

One misstep leads to eternal regret.

A single grave mistake can have lasting consequences. This saying urges mindfulness, especially when stakes are high.

众人拾柴火焰高

Zhòng rén shí chái huǒ yàn gāo

When many people gather firewood, the flames rise high.

Collaboration breeds strength. This proverb highlights the power of teamwork and collective effort in achieving great things.

吃一堑，长一智

Chī yī qiàn, zhǎng yī zhì
Fall into a pit, gain a bit of wisdom.
Every failure teaches a lesson. Life's stumbles are stepping stones to deeper understanding.

欲穷千里目，更上一层楼

Yù qióng qiān lǐ mù, gèng shàng yī céng lóu
To see a thousand miles farther, climb another floor.
To gain greater vision, one must elevate their perspective. This is both literal and metaphorical: grow, rise, and you'll see more.

巧妇难为无米之炊

Qiǎo fù nán wéi wú mǐ zhī chuī
Even the cleverest housewife cannot cook without rice.
Skill is not enough without resources. The proverb underscores the importance of preparation and support.

人心隔肚皮

Rén xīn gé dù pí

The human heart is hidden behind the belly.
We cannot see into others' true thoughts. Appearances
may be deceiving, so trust should be earned slowly.

一诺千金

Yī nuò qiān jīn

A promise worth a thousand pieces of gold.
A vow must be honored. This proverb speaks to the sacred
weight of one's word and the value of integrity.

狗嘴里吐不出象牙

Gǒu zuǐ lǐ tǔ bù chū xiàngyá

You can't get ivory from a dog's mouth.
Don't expect noble speech or behavior from ignoble
people. Character determines expression.

人怕出名猪怕壮

Rén pà chū míng, zhū pà zhuàng

A man fears fame, a pig fears fatness.
Fame invites trouble, just as fat pigs invite slaughter. This
proverb warns that attention can be dangerous.

路遥知马力，日久见人心

Lù yáo zhī mǎ lì, rì jiǔ jiàn rén xīn

Distance tests a horse's strength; time reveals a person's heart.

True character is proven over time and through hardship. Patience reveals the truth of both people and things.

鹬蚌相争，渔翁得利

Yù bàng xiāng zhēng, yúwēng dé lì

While the snipe and the clam fight, the fisherman profits.

While two sides struggle, a third may benefit. A timeless warning about conflict and opportunism.

不经一事，不长一智

Bù jīng yī shì, bù zhǎng yī zhì

Without experiencing a matter, you gain no wisdom.

Only through experience does true knowledge arise. Living is the classroom of wisdom.

兔死狐悲

Tù sǐ hú bēi

The fox mourns the rabbit's death.

Those of the same kind share fate. Seeing another's misfortune reminds us of our own vulnerability.

夜路走多了总会碰到鬼

Yè lù zǒu duō le zǒng huì pèng dào guǐ

If you walk too often at night, you'll eventually meet a ghost.

Constantly taking risks or doing wrong increases the chance of trouble. A warning about tempting fate.

将欲取之，必先予之

Jiāng yù qǔ zhī, bì xiān yǔ zhī

To take something, one must first offer something.

To achieve gain, one must first give. A strategic lesson in diplomacy, leadership, and generosity.

上梁不正下梁歪

Shàng liáng bù zhèng xià liáng wāi

If the upper beam is not straight, the lower beam will be crooked.

Leadership sets the tone. When those at the top falter, those below will follow. A call for moral example.

兵马未动，粮草先行

Bīng mǎ wèi dòng, liáng cǎo xiān xíng

Before the troops move, supplies must be prepared.
Preparation is the foundation of success. Plan thoroughly
before you act.

强龙难压地头蛇

Qiáng lóng nán yā dì tóu shé

Even a mighty dragon cannot suppress a local snake.
Local power, even if small, can resist outside force. A
pragmatic lesson in respect and strategy.

宁为鸡首，不为牛后

Nìng wéi jī shǒu, bù wéi niú hòu

Better to be the head of a chicken than the tail of an ox.
Better to lead in a small way than to follow in a big one.
Autonomy and agency matter more than scale.

君子报仇，十年不晚

Jūnzǐ bàochóu, shí nián bù wǎn

A noble person avenges at the right time, even if ten years
late.
True justice is patient, not impulsive. Righteous action
waits for the right moment.

有志者事竟成

Yǒu zhì zhě shì jìng chéng

Where there is will, the task will be accomplished.
With determination, anything is possible. Resolve fuels
success.

千里之行，始于足下

Qiān lǐ zhī xíng, shǐ yú zú xià

A journey of a thousand miles begins beneath one's feet.
All great endeavors start with a single step. Begin now,
however small the beginning may seem.

一山不容二虎

Yī shān bù róng èr hǔ

One mountain cannot contain two tigers.
Two strong personalities or powers cannot coexist in the
same domain. A lesson about rivalry and dominance.

滴水之恩，当涌泉相报

Dī shuǐ zhī ēn, dāng yǒng quán xiāng bào

A drop of kindness should be returned with a spring.

Gratitude should be abundant and heartfelt. Never forget the smallest kindness.

大器晚成

Dà qì wǎn chéng
A great vessel takes time to complete.
True greatness takes time to develop. Be patient with your journey and your gifts.

塞翁失马，焉知非福

Sài wēng shī mǎ, yān zhī fēi fú
The old man lost his horse—who knows if it's a blessing?
What seems like misfortune may hold hidden blessings. Life is unpredictable, and wisdom lies in staying open to all outcomes.

不怕慢，就怕站

Bù pà màn, jiù pà zhàn
Don't fear moving slowly, only standing still.
Progress—however slow—is better than stagnation. Keep going forward.

知足常乐

Zhī zú cháng lè

He who knows contentment will always be happy.
Gratitude and simplicity are the roots of lasting happiness.
Ambition without limits leads to restlessness.

风雨之后见彩虹

Fēng yǔ zhī hòu jiàn cǎihóng

After wind and rain comes the rainbow.
Hardship gives way to beauty. Endure the storm to reach the light.

宁静致远

Nìng jìng zhì yuǎn

Tranquility yields transcendence.
A calm mind sees clearly and reaches far. Inner peace is the seed of outer success.

举头三尺有神明

Jǔ tóu sān chǐ yǒu shén míng

Three feet above your head, the spirits watch.
Live with integrity—even when alone. The divine (or conscience) is always present.

读万卷书，行万里路

Dú wàn juàn shū, xíng wàn lǐ lù

Read ten thousand books, travel ten thousand miles.
Wisdom is found in both study and experience. One
without the other is incomplete.

百闻不如一见

Bǎi wén bù rú yī jiàn

Hearing a hundred times is not as good as seeing once.
Direct experience is more reliable than second-hand
knowledge. See for yourself.

种瓜得瓜，种豆得豆

Zhòng guā dé guā, zhòng dòu dé dòu
Plant melons, get melons; plant beans, get beans.
You reap what you sow. Actions have consequences, and
intentions shape results.

镜花水月

Jìng huā shuǐ yuè

Flowers in a mirror, moon on the water.
Beautiful illusions that cannot be grasped. A poetic
reminder that not all things are as they appear.

青出于蓝而胜于蓝

Qīng chū yú lán ér shèng yú lán
Indigo comes from the blue plant, yet surpasses it in color.
The student can surpass the master. Growth is not
betrayal—it is evolution.

光阴似箭，日月如梭

Guāng yīn sì jiàn, rì yuè rú suō
Time flies like an arrow; the sun and moon turn like a
spinning wheel.
Life passes swiftly. Use your time wisely and cherish each
moment.

良药苦口利于病

Liáng yào kǔ kǒu lì yú bìng
Good medicine tastes bitter but cures the illness.
Hard truths and difficult actions often bring healing and
growth. Don't avoid the unpleasant if it helps you heal.

前事不忘，后事之师

Qián shì bù wàng, hòu shì zhī shī
Do not forget the past—it is the teacher for the future.
History holds lessons. Learn from your experiences and
from those who came before.

一寸光阴**一寸金**，寸金难买寸光阴

Yī cùn guāng yīn yī cùn jīn, cùn jīn nán mǎi cùn guāng yīn

An inch of time is an inch of gold, but an inch of gold cannot buy an inch of time.

Time is the most valuable treasure. Spend it with purpose.

水能载舟，亦能覆舟

Shuǐ néng zài zhōu, yì néng fù zhōu

Water can carry a boat, but it can also overturn it.

What supports you can also destroy you. Power, people, and emotions must be respected.

天道酬勤

Tiān dào chóu qín

Heaven rewards the diligent.

Hard work is divinely favored. Persistent effort will be repaid, even if slowly.

About the Author

Maxwell W. Wilson is a passionate lifelong learner with a background in Information Technology and Contemporary Marketing. He believes that knowledge should be both enlightening and enjoyable—a philosophy he brings into every book he writes. For Maxwell, writing is more than just sharing information; it's about creating a journey where readers engage, learn, and have fun. His commitment to rigorous research ensures that every detail is spot-on, while his lively writing style keeps readers captivated. Whether you're diving into new concepts or brushing up on the familiar, Maxwell's books promise an experience that's both informative and refreshingly entertaining.

For a behind-the-scenes look at Maxwell's latest thoughts and projects, you can find him on Instagram under the handle **@anotsowiseoldman**.

Made in United States
Orlando, FL
02 July 2025

62551530R00020